AF228394

1 & 2
CORINTHIANS

1 & 2 CORINTHIANS

Rob Wynalda, Joel R. Beeke,
and Paul M. Smalley

REFORMATION HERITAGE BOOKS

Grand Rapids, Michigan

Reformation Heritage Books
3070 29th St. SE
Grand Rapids, MI 49512
616-977-0889
orders@heritagebooks.org
www.heritagebooks.org

25 26 27 28 29 30/11 10 9 8 7 6 5 4 3 2

ISBN 979-8-88686-169-3

PREFACE

In Deuteronomy 17, Moses leaves final instructions concerning the future of Israel. As a prophet of God, he foretells that Israel will set a king over the nation (v. 14). This king must be an Israelite, not a foreigner (v. 15), and is forbidden to do certain things (vv. 16–17). In verse 18, Moses transitions to what the king should do. The king is commanded not to simply acquire a copy of the law (the entire book of Deuteronomy), but to handwrite his own copy of the law. The purpose was so that he would read it, fear the Lord, obey, avoid pride, not deviate, and enjoy a long reign (vv. 19–20; cf. Prov. 4:20–27).

More than three thousand years later, modern educators have discovered that students who write out notes by hand have a much higher retention rate than those who simply hear or visually read the information. Apparently, God knew this to be true for the kings of Israel also.

This series of books, known as The Bible Journal, was born from the insight found in Deuteronomy 17:18. Your Bible Journal gives you the opportunity to write out your own copy of a portion of the Holy Scriptures, just as the ancient kings of Israel were instructed to do. Writing out the words of the Bible helps a person to engage the Word of God by slowing down the process of reading the text. Writing answers to the discussion questions also helps you to thoughtfully engage the text. Furthermore, by completing a journal, you leave a legacy to pass on to future generations your insights and personal applications of the text (Deut. 6:6–9; Ps. 78:4–7).

To prepare you to meditate on this portion of the Holy Scriptures, we include an introduction to the book of the Bible to help you understand more thoroughly the Bible book you are about to write out in full. Study Questions and Devotional Reflections have been added after the blank pages set aside for copying each chapter of God's Word. The Study Questions focus on individual verses to keep you thinking about what you are writing, and the Devotional Reflections are designed to help you focus on a few of the major takeaways for your practical Christian life that each Bible chapter provides. We wish to thank Reformation Heritage Books for allowing us to use material drawn from *The Reformation Heritage KJV Study Bible* for the Bible Introduction material and for the Devotional Reflections. The Study Questions have been written by the authors of *The Bible Journal*. Thus, The Bible Journal walks you through a process of getting acquainted with a book of the Bible, copying a chapter by hand, reflecting on the meaning and application of that chapter, and then repeating the process for the next chapter. Families, friends, and small groups can work through a journal together, discussing their meditations for mutual edification as guided by the discussion questions.

The mass production of the Bible since the invention of the printing press has greatly blessed the world. However, there is also great benefit for Bible readers of all ages in following the Deuteronomy 17:18 principle and producing your own handwritten copy of the text.

May God richly bless you in writing and learning His Word through The Bible Journal (Rom. 1:16).

—Rob Wynalda, Joel R. Beeke, and Paul M. Smalley

Introduction to the Book of
1 CORINTHIANS

AUTHORSHIP: The apostle Paul identifies himself as the author (1:1), and there is no compelling reason to doubt the claim. The vocabulary, theology, and personal information all point to the legitimacy of Pauline authorship.

DATE: Paul wrote the letter while at Ephesus before the celebration of Pentecost (16:8). He planted the church in Corinth in AD 51 and stayed in the city for "a good while" (Acts 18:18). The next year he went on to Ephesus where he stayed for almost three years. During the latter part of his time in Ephesus he wrote 1 Corinthians, placing the date in the spring of either AD 54 or 55.

THEME: Boasting or glorying in God, which promotes unity in the body as well as purity in both doctrine and behavior.

PURPOSE: (1) To respond to a letter from the Corinthian believers asking questions on various topics (marriage and divorce, food offered to idols, decorum in public worship, spiritual gifts, and the collection), and (2) to address the troubling reports he heard from those of Chloe's household informing him of the divisions that existed within the church and threatened the unity of the body and, therefore, brought reproach to God's glory.

SYNOPSIS
The Contribution of 1 Corinthians to Redemptive Revelation
After Paul endured beatings in Philippi (Acts 16) and scorn in Athens (Acts 17), he traveled to Corinth (Acts 18) "in weakness, and in fear, and in much trembling" (1 Cor. 2:3). He began preaching in the synagogue every Sabbath (Acts 18:4) and after opposition from the Jews he turned his focus to preaching the gospel to the Gentiles. Despite the discouragement of the opposition, Paul saw fruit from the preaching of the gospel. Crispus, the chief ruler of the synagogue, believed on Christ and many Corinthians heard and believed. Paul received greater

confidence and encouragement directly from the Lord, who exhorted the apostle not to be afraid, but to speak, "for I am with thee, and no man shall set on thee to hurt thee: for I have much people in this city" (Acts 18:10). Paul remained in Corinth for eighteen months teaching them. Apollos ministered in Corinth after Paul had gone on to Ephesus. Certainly because of the time Paul spent, as well as the ministry of Apollos and even Peter, Paul expected the Corinthian believers to be more mature in their walk with God than was evidenced by the reports and questions that came to him (as seen in the letter's repeated refrain, "know ye not?" [1 Cor. 3:16; 5:6; 6:2–3, 9, 15–16, 19; 9:13, 24]).

Given the nature of the sordid behavior for which Paul must confront the Corinthian believers, the letter surprisingly begins with numerable commendations and thanksgiving to God for the grace shown to the church at Corinth. Paul identifies them as the church of God, sanctified in Christ, and called to be saints (1:2). This greeting sets the basis for how Paul will confront them throughout the book. They are God's church, set apart by God in Christ to be saints. Therefore, they are to live as God's people, as gospel people. Rather than boasting in themselves, they are to boast in God (1:31; 3:21; 4:7). They are not to live for themselves but for God's glory in all things (10:31), and for the good of others with love governing all their words, thoughts, and actions (ch. 13). In the opening greetings and thanksgiving Paul genuinely praises God for the work of grace in them and urges them to continue to pursue Christ so that they might be blameless in the day of the Lord Jesus Christ (1:8).

After the opening verses Paul immediately draws focus onto the report he has heard, namely, that of divisions in the church (1:18–6:20). There were those in the church who were encouraging a party spirit, rallying around Paul, Apollos, Cephas (Peter), and even a party that claimed to be of Christ. Given that these men preached the same gospel and their teachings were not antithetical one to another, the nature of the party spirit was not theological, but one of personality. Paul objects to the disunity by enumerating the glories of the gospel of Jesus Christ. Though foolish, offensive, and weak from man's natural perspective, the gospel is the wisdom and power of God and it is through the preaching of the cross that God has demonstrated His glory. Paul builds his argument to its culminating point by announcing that believers are by God in union with Christ, who of God was made unto us wisdom, that is, our righteousness, sanctification, and redemption (1:30). Jesus Christ is everything to and for the believer with the result that all glory is due to God alone. A divisive party spirit is antithetical to the gospel of Jesus Christ. Paul goes on to show that the nature of gospel ministry (chs. 3–4) also eradicates the acceptability of having a party spirit.

Not only was there a divisive spirit among the church, there was also immorality so odious that the Gentiles did not even name it (ch. 5). What was so grieving to Paul was not merely the fact that one within the church would be involved in an illicit relation with his father's wife (5:1), but that the church tolerated it! He exhorts them to deal with the sin and deliver such a one over to Satan and he rebukes them for glorying in the sin itself. Again, the gospel forms the basis of Paul's argumentation. Christ is our Passover (5:7). In Christ all things are new. The old is to be put away and believers are not to be holding on to the former things of malice and wickedness, but rather are to live in sincerity and truth (5:8). In Christ they are sanctified, set apart. Therefore, they are to live accordingly.

Next, Paul addresses the report that there were scandalous litigations between church members (ch. 6). The Corinthians boasted in themselves about how spiritual they were. Yet, they could not even resolve differences between themselves. They took their differences before the unbelievers to find resolution (6:6). Paul encourages them that it is better to accept the wrong and the loss than it is to bring reproach to Christ's name (6:7).

Chapters 7–16 form the second major division of the book. In these chapters Paul addresses issues raised by the Corinthian church. Chapter 7 focuses on the subject of marriage and divorce. Chapters 8–10 touch upon food offered to idols and how to deal with fellow church members whose consciences vary on these matters. Paul provides a personal illustration in chapter 9, showing the difference between rights and liberty. As an apostle he has the right to receive remuneration for his labors, but for the sake of his testimony and for the usefulness of his ministry he has the liberty to refuse it. Chapter 11 focuses on decorum in public worship with respect to gender distinctions and the Lord's Supper. Chapters 12–14 provide the most detailed treatment of the spiritual gifts in the New Testament, which Paul frames around love for the brethren and orderly worship. While much of the focus in this letter focuses on purity of life, we see in chapter 15 that Christians are to be pure in doctrine as well. Paul's in-depth treatment of the resurrection of Christ and of believers highlights the point that belief is a matter of morality and motivation for the Christian life (15:58). Finally, Paul addresses the matter of the collection for the saints. He closes his letter by mentioning his travel plans and final exhortations to stand fast in the faith (16:13).

Paul's first letter addresses many issues that are relevant for the church today and he wisely shows believers how to apply the gospel to the everyday circumstances of life.

OUTLINE

I. Introduction (1:1–9)
   A. Greeting (1:1–3)
   B. Thanksgiving (1:4–9)

II. Solutions to Problems Reported (1:10–6:20)
   A. The Problem of Division (1:10–4:21)
      1. Divisions in the Church (1:10–17)
      2. The Gospel of Christ Resolves Division (1:18–3:4)
      3. The Nature of Gospel Ministry Resolves Division (3:5–4:21)

   B. The Problems of Scandalous Sins (5:1–6:20)
      1. Failure to Discipline Sin (5:1–13)
      2. Litigation between Church Members (6:1–8)
      3. Sin, the Kingdom, and Salvation (6:9–11)
      4. Sexual Promiscuity (6:12–20)

III. Answers to Questions from Corinthian Church (7:1–16:4)
   A. Concerning Marriage, Divorce, the Unmarried, and Widows (7:1–40)
   B. Concerning Conscience regarding Meat Offered to Idols (8:1–11:1)
      1. Importance of Conscience (8:1–13)
      2. Personal Illustration from Apostolic Rights (9:1–27)
      3. Warnings against Idolatry and Call to Glorify God (10:1–11:1)

   C. Concerning Decorum in Public Worship (11:2–34)
      1. Headship and Headcoverings (11:2–16)
      2. Behavior at the Lord's Supper (11:17–34)

   D. Concerning the Spiritual Gifts (12:1–14:40)
      1. Unity in Diversity in the One Body (12:1–31)
      2. Preeminence of Love (13:1–13)
      3. Prophecy and Tongues, Decency and Order (14:1–40)

Notes

1

2

3

4

5

6

7

8

Notes

9

10

11

12

13

14

15

16

Notes

17

18

19

20

21

22

23

Notes

24

25

26

27

28

29

30

31

STUDY QUESTIONS

1. Verse 2: What do we learn about the church here?

2. Verses 8–9: What is promised to God's saints? Why can we be sure of it?

3. Verse 10: What is Paul's concern for the Corinthian saints?

4. Verses 12–13: Why is it wrong for Christians to split into factions following different leaders?

5. Verse 18: How do different people perceive the gospel?

6. Verse 21: How much does human wisdom help people to know God?

7. Verse 24: What enables people to believe the gospel of Christ crucified?

8. Verses 27–29: Whom has God chosen, for the most part? Why?

9. Verse 30: What has God made Christ to be for those in Him? How do we experience that?

DEVOTIONAL REFLECTIONS

1. Meditate upon God's objective act of setting you apart in Christ Jesus. If you have been sanctified in Christ, what are the ramifications and implications of that reality for your daily life, family life, and church life?

2. Do you consistently find hope and satisfaction in the gospel of Christ's life, death, and resurrection? What are warning signs that someone is being taken up with or enamored by the wisdom of this world?

3. We are all boasters. Paul does not rebuke the Corinthian church for boasting or glorying, but for boasting and glorying in the wrong thing. Do you consciously boast in God's saving work and His grace in sending His own Son to the cross, or are you glorying in your own talents, gifts, and graces?

Notes

1

2

3

4

5

6

7

8

Notes

9

10

11

12

13

14

Notes

15

16

STUDY QUESTIONS

1. Verses 1–2: What was Paul determined not to do in his preaching? What did he preach?

2. Verse 4: What made Paul's preaching effective?

3. Verse 7: How does Paul describe his message?

4. Verses 9–10: How do human beings know God's secret purposes?

5. Verse 14: How does a natural man (lacking God's Spirit) respond to God's Word?

6. Verse 16: What do believers have? What does that mean (Rom. 12:2; Eph. 4:23; Phil. 2:5)?

DEVOTIONAL REFLECTIONS

1. This chapter teaches the necessity of the Holy Spirit's work in illuminating you to discern the gospel. If you are a believer in Christ, why should that truth motivate you to praise God?

2. Paul says that those who have received the Spirit are able to judge all things. Do you live daily in the awareness that the Spirit guides you? How can you evaluate all things in the light of the Spirit's ministry in your life?

3. Pray for the help of the Holy Spirit each time you open the Word, asking for guidance as you meditate on the Word, both personally and with family.

Notes

1

2

3

4

5

6

Notes

7

8

9

10

11

12

13

Notes

14

15

16

17

18

19

20

21

Notes

22

23

STUDY QUESTIONS

1. Verses 1–2: What does Paul call the Corinthians? What does this mean?

2. Verses 5–7: Why is it foolish to glory in human ministers of the gospel?

3. Verse 10: How does Paul describe the work of starting and developing a church?

4. Verse 11: Who is the foundation of the church? What does that imply about preaching?

5. Verse 15: What will happen to a gospel minister if God judges his work to be lacking?

6. Verses 16–17: What does Paul say about the church and those who do it harm?

7. Verse 21–23: What does Paul mean by "all things are yours" (see Matt. 28:18; Rom. 8:28)?

DEVOTIONAL REFLECTIONS

1. How do you view your minister? Do you pray for the minister(s) that God has given to you?

2. Talk through the significance of what it means that all things belong to believers in Christ (v. 22) and how that corrects worldly notions of entitlement.

3. If believers are the temple of God corporately, how should we live our lives? Pursuing holiness does not just benefit individuals, but has a corporate effect.

Notes

1

2

3

4

5

6

Notes

7

8

9

10

11

12

Notes

13

14

15

16

17

18

19

Notes

20

21

STUDY QUESTIONS

1. Verse 1: How should we view the ministers of Christ?

2. Verses 3–5: Why was Paul relatively unconcerned about how people judged him?

3. Verse 7: Why should no one boast of being different from others?

4. Verses 9–13: How are the apostles the opposite of what we would expect from great leaders?

5. Verses 15–16: Why should the Corinthian saints love and imitate Paul?

6. Verse 20: What does Paul teach about God's kingdom here?

DEVOTIONAL REFLECTIONS

1. Consider your daily need of grace to grow in godliness. Learn from Paul's warning to the Corinthian church that we will not ever be at a place in this life where we can say, "I have finally arrived spiritually." What reminders have you had lately that you have not yet arrived?

2. Consider in your mind and with your family that all you and they have and are comes from God, and praise Him for His goodness and kindness.

Notes

1

2

3

4

5

6

Notes

7

8

9

10

11

12

Notes

13

STUDY QUESTIONS

1. Verses 1–2: What sin was being tolerated in the Corinthian church?

2. Verses 4–5: What should the church do with this unrepentant sinner in its membership?

3. Verse 7: What did Paul say about the Passover? What is the similarity (Ex. 12:1–13)?

4. Verses 9–10: Why can't Christians separate from all sinners?

5. Verse 11: What sins does Paul list (among others) as requiring a break in church fellowship?

DEVOTIONAL REFLECTIONS

1. Consider the sobering effects of sin. What are some examples of how sin not only affects the one who commits the sin, but also those who are connected to him or her, both family and church?

2. Meditate on the guilt-removing and life-transforming work of Christ's sacrifice. He is the true Passover, or Deliverer from bondage. If you are in Christ, things are fundamentally different. This reality ought to be remembered daily and depended upon experientially.

Chapter 6

1

2

3

4

5

6

7

Notes

8

9

10

11

12

13

Notes

14

15

16

17

18

19

20

STUDY QUESTIONS

1. Verse 1: What problem does Paul address in this section of his epistle?

2. Verses 4–5: How should believers seek to resolve their conflicts with each other?

3. Verses 9–10: What warning does Paul make concerning God's kingdom?

4. Verse 11: How can people who have committed the sins just listed inherit the kingdom?

5. Verse 15: Why is it such a great sin for Christians to engage in fornication?

6. Verses 19–20: How should believers view their bodies? How should they live?

DEVOTIONAL REFLECTIONS

1. If there has been a wrong done, how do you pursue reconciliation with another believer in your church or another member in your family?

2. How does the believer's union with Christ affect his or her daily living? Chapter 6 works out in detail the relationship between doctrine and practice. Paul draws the reader's attention to objective truths, or indicatives: you have been washed, you have been sanctified, you have been justified, your bodies are members of Christ, and your body is the temple of the Holy Ghost. He then gives a command: flee fornication. What is the relationship between what you are in Christ and the importance of purity?

Notes

1

2

3

4

5

6

7

Notes

8

9

10

11

12

13

14

Notes

15

16

17

18

19

20

21

Notes

22

23

24

25

26

27

28

Notes

29

30

31

32

33

34

Notes

35

36

37

38

39

40

STUDY QUESTIONS

1. Verse 2: What is God's ordinary means of protecting people from committing fornication?

2. Verse 5: What instruction does Paul give to married couples?

3. Verse 9: What is one reason someone should seek to get married?

4. Verses 12–14: What should a Christian do if he or she is married to an unbeliever? Why?

5. Verse 15: What does this teach about divorce?

6. Verse 19: How can Paul say this, given that circumcision was God's commandment (Gal. 5:6; 6:15; Col. 2:11–13; 3:11)?

7. Verse 22: How should belonging to Christ change the way we see slavery and freedom?

8. Verses 26–28: What advice did Paul give to believers in a time of great distress?

9. Verse 31: What does Paul teach about this world? How should that affect how we use it?

10. Verses 32–34: How can being unmarried allow for serving the Lord with less distraction?

11. Verse 39: What is the Christian's liberty and limitation in choosing a spouse?

DEVOTIONAL REFLECTIONS

1. The grace of Christian contentment pervades Paul's entire argument. Are you enjoying contentment in your current calling? If single, are you content? If married, are you contentedly relating to your spouse in selfless ways?

2. God's providential orchestration of your circumstances is His will for you. How do you factor in God's providence in your decision-making process?

Notes

1

2

3

4

5

6

Notes

7

8

9

10

11

Notes

12

13

STUDY QUESTIONS

1. Verse 1: How might knowledge be dangerous?

2. Verse 4: What is the basic Christian response to the gods and idols of this world?

3. Verse 6: What does Paul teach about the Father and Christ? How does that support the doctrine of the Trinity?

4. Verses 8–9: How might Christians abuse their liberty to eat whatever food they choose?

5. Verse 12: If we sin against brothers and sisters in Christ, whom else do we wrong?

DEVOTIONAL REFLECTIONS

1. How do you view Christian liberty? As something that you have to do? Do you couple your knowledge regarding liberties with love for the brethren?

2. If Christ died for the believer with a weak conscience, how should we view such a person? The reality of the atonement ought to govern and dictate how believers view each other.

3. Consider all that you know by God's grace. Why is it important that your knowledge be coupled with love?

Notes

1

2

3

4

5

6

7

8

Notes

9

10

11

12

13

14

Notes

15

16

17

18

19

20

Notes

21

22

23

24

25

26

27

STUDY QUESTIONS

1. Verses 1–2: What does Paul imply here about the basis and evidence of being an apostle?

2. Verse 5: What right did the apostles have?

3. Verses 7–11: What arguments does Paul make that ministers should be financially supported?

4. Verses 13–14: How does the Old Testament priesthood confirm the support of ministers?

5. Verse 19: What approach did Paul take to evangelism?

6. Verses 20–22: What did Paul mean by becoming "all things to all men"?

7. Verses 24–25: How is the Christian life like a race or other athletic competition?

8. Verse 27: What are some ways that Christians should keep their bodies in subjection?

DEVOTIONAL REFLECTIONS

1. Do you love your liberties more than you love your brothers? Paul openly acknowledged the liberties and rights he had as an apostle and minister of the gospel. Yet, he was willing to set his liberties aside for the sake of something greater, the gospel of Jesus Christ.

2. Are you running the Christian race? If so, how does the Christian race play itself out in your life and in the lives of your family members? How are you showing that the gospel of Jesus Christ reigns supreme in your affections as you seek to run the race before you?

Notes

Chapter 10

1

2

3

4

5

6

7

8

9

Notes

10

11

12

13

14

15

16

17

Notes

18

19

20

21

22

23

24

25

26

Notes

27

28

29

30

31

32

33

STUDY QUESTIONS

1. Verses 1–5: How were Israel's experiences somewhat like baptism and the Lord's Supper? How is that a warning to members of the Christian church?

2. Verses 6–10: What are some of Israel's sins that we should be careful to avoid?

3. Verse 11: What is one purpose of the Old Testament history of Israel?

4. Verse 13: What encouragements does this offer to the tempted? How does it encourage you?

5. Verse 16: What takes place when believers partake of the Lord's Supper?

6. Verses 20–21: What does Paul teach about idol worship? Why should Christians avoid it?

7. Verse 23: How is this a helpful principle for making decisions (1 Cor. 6:12)?

8. Verses 25–26: Why are Christians generally free to enjoy the good things of this world?

9. Verse 31: What should be our ultimate goal in all that we do?

10. Verses 32–33: What is an important way we seek the goal of verse 31?

DEVOTIONAL REFLECTIONS

1. Paul applies the Old Testament history to our lives to show the importance of persevering in the faith. It is not enough to experience the external benefits of the visible church. There must be the experiential application of God's grace in the soul. Reflect on how a spiritual privilege is not the same as a spiritual possession.

2. Paul encourages discernment (determining the spiritual profit of a thing) and love (determining whether something builds up) in deciding questions relating to liberty. How does this work itself out in your life and in the life of your family? How does God's glory and others' good play into the exercise of what you do and do not do?

Notes

Chapter 11

1

2

3

4

5

6

7

8

Notes

9

10

11

12

13

14

15

16

17

Notes

18

19

20

21

22

23

24

Notes

25

26

27

28

29

30

31

32

Notes

33

34

STUDY QUESTIONS

1. Verse 1: Why is it good to be a "follower" (or "imitator") of people who imitate Christ?

2. Verses 4–5: What does Paul say about covering the head in worship?

3. Verses 8–9: What does Paul observe from the creation of man and woman (Genesis 2)?

4. Verses 11–12: What does Paul remind us about men and women here?

5. Verses 14–15: What does nature teach us about the hair of men and women?

6. Verse 16: Why might Paul appeal to the custom of "the churches of God"?

7. Verses 20–22: How were the Corinthians despising the church and the Lord's Supper?

8. Verses 23–26: What is the meaning of the Lord's Supper?

9. Verse 28: What responsibility does a person have before taking the Lord's Supper?

10. Verses 30–32: What might God do to a church that dishonors His sacred ordinances?

11. Verse 34: Why should Christians act at church differently from at home?

DEVOTIONAL REFLECTIONS

1. When you come to the house of God for corporate worship, how you conduct yourself matters. Paul argues for proper decorum in public worship according to God's created order. When you enter His house for worship, how should you act in a way that honors the glory and will of the Lord?

2. God has blessed His people with wonderful tokens of His love such as the Lord's Supper. Here Christians celebrate the union they have with Christ and with one another in Christ. This is a time for self-examination and is therefore serious. It is a sign and seal of Christ's atoning work by which the believer is nourished and strengthened in his faith in God's promises.

Notes

1

2

3

4

5

6

7

8

9

Notes

10

11

12

13

14

15

Notes

16

17

18

19

20

21

22

23

Notes

24

25

26

27

28

29

Notes

30

31

STUDY QUESTIONS

1. Verse 3: What is impossible without the work of the Holy Spirit?

2. Verses 4–6: How is the Trinity involved in spiritual gifts (on "Lord" and "God," see 8:6)?

3. Verse 7: What is the nature and purpose of spiritual gifts?

4. Verse 10: What is the gift of "tongues" (Acts 2:1–11)?

5. Verse 11: How does this verse prove that the Holy Spirit is God and that He is a person?

6. Verse 12: What does Paul teach about Christ's church as a "body"?

7. Verses 15–17: Why do all believers belong to the body, though some believers are not the same as others?

8. Verse 21: Why do we need Christians who are different from us?

9. Verse 26: What results from the oneness of Christ's body?

10. Verses 29–30: What is the implied answer to these questions? Why is that important?

DEVOTIONAL REFLECTIONS

1. God graciously gives gifts to each of His children. He sovereignly decides who receives what gift and how many. Often Christians become discouraged because they do not have the same gift as someone else. Others can become proud because of the gifts that they have as though they earned them. God's sovereign giving of gifts should evoke praise and thanksgiving rather than discouragement, and instill humility because the gifts were granted according to God's will and not the receiver's merit. When considering your gift, do so with a God-centered perspective rather than a self-centered one.

2. Paul highlights the unity of the church in his discussion of the spiritual gifts. He describes this unity by reminding believers that when one suffers, all suffer. And when one is honored, all rejoice. In many ways, it is easier to suffer alongside another who is suffering. It is not always easy to rejoice when another is honored. What is your response when someone else is honored and you feel overlooked? Are you able to rejoice with them? How can we dissipate envying and jealousy in our churches and in our homes?

Notes

1

2

3

4

5

6

7

8

Notes

9

10

11

12

13

STUDY QUESTIONS

1. Verses 1–3: What is true of us if we lack love (KJV, charity), even though we are greatly gifted?

2. Verses 4–7: How does love move people to act? How do you need to change your actions?

3. Verses 8–10: What is one way that love surpasses these spiritual gifts?

4. Verse 12: How will our knowledge change when Christ returns?

5. Verse 13: What are the three great Christian virtues?

DEVOTIONAL REFLECTIONS

1. Love is to govern all of our motives. Examine whether all you say, know, and do is governed by love. What sins against love do you need to confess?

2. Paul describes love in various action verbs. It has often been said that we can replace the word "charity" with the name "Christ" and see more clearly God's grace to us in His Son. Christ acts toward us in all these ways. It is only through Christ that you will ever be able to have and show true love.

Notes

Chapter 14

1

2

3

4

5

6

Notes

7

8

9

10

11

12

13

14

Notes

15

16

17

18

19

20

21

Notes

22

23

24

25

26

27

Notes

28

29

30

31

32

33

34

35

36

Notes

37

38

39

40

STUDY QUESTIONS

1. Verse 1: What is prophecy (Luke 1:70; Acts 21:9–11)?

2. Verses 2–3: Why was prophecy superior to speaking in tongues?

3. Verses 8–9: What does this imply about the language(s) used in a worship service?

4. Verse 12: What should be our goal in all that we do in the church?

5. Verse 14: How much did the person speaking in tongues understand of his words?

6. Verse 19: How did speaking in tongues in church compare to speaking in a known language?

7. Verse 20: How should we be like children? How should we be like adults?

8. Verse 23: What would a visitor think if everyone in church were speaking in tongues?

9. Verses 27–28: What other gift was needed for speaking in tongues to edify the church?

10. Verses 31–32: Were people who prophesied in an ecstatic state out of their own control?

11. Verse 33: What does this teach us about God? About public worship?

12. Verse 37: What did Paul say about his writings? What does that imply about Scripture?

13. Verse 40: What principle should be followed in the church? Why is this important?

DEVOTIONAL REFLECTIONS

1. Within the context of prophecy and tongues, Paul highlights the importance of decent and orderly worship. When the church gathers in God's presence, believers are to engage in worship seriously and reverently. How do Paul's exhortations in this chapter teach you how to frame your focus when you enter into God's house?

2. As you consider your spiritual gifts, is your focus more on the gift from a self-centered perspective or from the perspective of love for the brethren and desire to edify, encourage, and build up the brethren? How can you put your gifts to work in a way that glorifies God and edifies the body?

Notes

1

2

3

4

5

6

7

8

Notes

9

10

11

12

13

14

15

16

Notes

17

18

19

20

21

22

23

24

25

Notes

26

27

28

29

30

31

32

Notes

33

34

35

36

37

38

39

40

Notes

41

42

43

44

45

46

47

48

Notes

49

50

51

52

53

54

55

Notes

56

57

58

STUDY QUESTIONS

1. Verse 1: Look up the word "gospel." What does it mean?

2. Verses 3–4: How does Paul summarize the gospel?

3. Verses 5–8: Why is it significant that Christ appeared to many people after His resurrection?

4. Verse 10: What was the source of Paul's character and labor?

5. Verses 13–15: If there is no resurrection, what does that imply for Christianity?

6. Verses 16–19: What else would be true if there is no resurrection of the dead?

7. Verse 20: What are "firstfruits"? How does this apply to Christ?

8. Verses 21–22: How does Paul compare Adam and Christ?

9. Verse 23: When will Christ raise His people from the dead?

10. Verse 26: What does Paul teach about death here? What does that mean?

11. Verse 28: What will it mean for God to be "all in all" (see Rev. 21:3, 11, 23)?

12. Verse 32: If we had no resurrection hope, how would we live differently?

13. Verses 36–37: What does Paul's illustration about planting a seed show us about death and resurrection?

14. Verses 42–44: What are the differences between the believer's body now and after the resurrection (on "spiritual," see Gal. 6:1)?

15. Verse 45: What does it mean to call Christ "the last Adam" (see Rom. 5:15–17; 1 Cor. 15: 21–22)?

16. Verses 47–49: How are Adam and Christ different? How will that affect Christ's people?

17. Verses 51–53: What will happen to believers who are still alive when Christ comes?

18. Verses 54–55: What Scripture passages is Paul quoting?

19. Verse 58: How should the doctrine of the resurrection affect how we serve the Lord?

DEVOTIONAL REFLECTIONS

1. The New Testament writers often pointed believers to the hope of the resurrection. The reality of Christ's bodily resurrection assures them that God the Father accepted the sacrifice made by God the Son. Because Jesus Christ was raised, dear believer, you can know with certainty that sin no longer holds dominion over you. The risen Lord reigns and rules over all, and all things have been put under His feet. How can you make sure you don't live as those who are "of all men most miserable" (v. 19)?

2. Because Jesus was raised and all those in Him will one day receive a body like His glorified body, your labors are not in vain. Consider how this truth should motivate you as you live before God each day in all the various spheres of service God has called you to: in the home, in the church, in the workplace.

Notes

1

2

3

4

5

6

7

8

Notes

9

10

11

12

13

14

15

16

Notes

17

18

19

20

21

22

23

24

STUDY QUESTIONS

1. Verses 1–2: What order did Paul give to the churches? What does that teach about the first day of the week?

2. Verses 8–9: Why did Paul plan to stay in Ephesus for a while?

3. Verses 10–11: What did Paul command regarding Timothy? Why?

4. Verses 13–14: What five things did Paul require of them? What do these mean?

5. Verses 15–16: How should Christians treat those who labor in gospel ministry?

6. Verse 19: What can we learn from "the churches of Asia" greeting the Corinthians?

7. Verse 22: What did Paul say about those who do not love Christ?

DEVOTIONAL REFLECTIONS

1. The collection for the saints in Jerusalem reminds us that the church of Jesus Christ is one church. Throughout the book Paul focuses on unity within the local church. It is not just the local church that is to be one, but also the universal, visible church. While it is not possible to meet every need of every believer in the world, Christians ought to have a broader vision of the kingdom of God on earth and seek to help in any way they are able. In what ways can you and your family meet needs outside your own local church?

2. The words "Anathema" (cursed by God) and "Maranatha" (our Lord is coming) (v. 22) bring us to the very edge of eternity. Ask yourself which word applies to you. The great line of division is between those who love Christ and those who do not. Believer, Christ bore your curse and now you long for His coming. Unbeliever, the curse is still resting upon you. You need to repent and seek Christ or He will appear as your justly condemning Judge.

<h1 style="text-align:center">Introduction to the Book of
2 CORINTHIANS</h1>

AUTHORSHIP: The apostle Paul claims to be the author (1:1), and there is no evidence to dispute this claim. The only section in the letter to come under dispute is 6:14–7:1. The objections to Pauline authorship on this section are not substantial enough to cast doubt. Second Corinthians is clearly one of the most personal of all Paul's letters and, therefore, there is no reason to question the legitimacy of Paul's authorship.

DATE: Paul wrote from Macedonia (7:5; 8:1; 9:2) about a year after writing 1 Corinthians, placing the timing of the letter in AD 56.

THEME: The nature of new covenant ministry: by the power of the Spirit, with present suffering, and for future glory.

PURPOSE: To defend Paul's ministry and message. Paul's ministry came under severe attack from two main vantage points. *First*, his message was viewed to be insufficient, and *second*, his ministry was characterized by weakness and suffering. While his opponents appear to be embarrassed by the apostle's suffering and subsequently reject Paul's ministry, Paul shows that suffering is a crucial part of advancing the glory of God. This is a book to which not only gospel ministers, but all Christians, can go to find encouragement and perspective in the midst of the difficulties of criticism, inadequacy, and insufficiency. Rather than give a false sense of self-worth, Paul bluntly affirms the insufficiency of any new covenant minister, but Christians may rejoice because their sufficiency is of God in all areas of life.

SYNOPSIS

The Contribution of 2 Corinthians to Redemptive Revelation
The book begins with an opening salutation that is common in letters of Paul's day (1:1–2). As he did in 1 Corinthians, he reminds the church that he is an apostle according to God's will. His apostleship has been called into question and they considered Paul an embarrassment

given the many evidences of weakness and suffering he endured. The Corinthian church continued to be enamored with evidences of success and triumph in ministry. Paul did not appear to be a Spirit-empowered success story. Despite the personal attacks Paul received, he offers thanksgiving to God, the Father of mercies, and the God of all comfort (1:3). He thanks the church for their prayers during times of persecution (v. 11).

Following the introductory elements of the letter, Paul immediately addresses his travel plans and why his plans changed (1:12–2:13). Some in the church accused Paul of vacillating in his travel plans, announcing his plans and then changing them without cause. He explains that his desire was to be a benefit to them (2:15), yet he decided not to come rather than cause such grief as he did in his prior visit (vv. 1–4). He chose instead to write them and tell them how much he loved them (v. 4).

Paul then turns his attention to a defense of his ministry (2:14–7:16). New covenant ministry in this present age does not always appear to be triumphant, but is often characterized by suffering. Some Corinthians often confused the future benefits of the kingdom with the present. Paul wrote that sufferings and trials do not contradict God's will in the present. God chose weak and earthen vessels to communicate His gospel so that it would be unmistakably clear that the power of the gospel is of God and not of ministers (4:7). The present weakness and trials are not the final story. The light affliction is but for a moment and believers look forward to a far greater, eternal weight of glory (v. 17). Holding together "the already" dimension of redemption along with the "not yet" blessings of redemption gives balance to Christians and ministers as they experience difficulties and trials in this present age. Within his discussion of the ministry, Paul unfolds the superiority of new covenant ministry by comparing it to the ministry of the old covenant (ch. 3). The glory of the new covenant ministry resides in the person of Jesus Christ, who has come and fulfilled His redemptive work. Christ is everything in this new covenant ministry. Christ's love motivates the minister to endure trials, even rejection. The reality that Christ died and rose again compelled Paul to preach reconciliation (5:11–21).

Paul encourages the Corinthian church to complete the giving that was begun earlier for the saints in Jerusalem (chs. 8–9). He tells them that the Macedonians have given generously despite their own trial of afflictions and poverty (8:1–5). Paul instructs the church regarding the manner in which it ought to give. Each person should purpose in his heart to give not out of guilt or necessity, or even grudgingly, but cheerfully (9:7). All generous giving is in grateful response to God's unspeakable gift (v. 15).

Paul's tone shifts in chs. 10–13. In this section he addresses his opponents directly, sharply challenging them. Some condemned Paul for being bold in his letters and weak when present (ch. 10). They boasted in themselves and compared themselves to others, seeking to show their own superiority (vv. 12–18). Paul turns the table on his opponents and requests that they bear with him as he engages in the folly of boasting (11:1). Paul's boast is different than theirs. He boasts in his weakness, because it is in weakness that God's strength is on display. Paul would rather glory in his infirmities in order that the power of Christ would rest on him (12:9–11). He brings his point home by telling them that he is willing to spend and be spent for their sakes because he loves them, even if it means they love him less (v. 15). He closes his letter with final exhortations, a warm demonstration of love, and a gracious doxology.

OUTLINE

I. Introduction (1:1–11)
    A. Greetings (1:1–2)
    B. Blessings to God for Comfort in Afflictions (1:3–11)

II. Defense of Travel Plans (1:12–2:13)
    A. Defense of Personal Integrity (1:12–24)
    B. Defense of Changed Plans (2:1–13)

III. Defense of Ministry (2:14–7:16)
    A. Message of Christ: Savor of Death and Life (2:14–17)
    B. People as Paul's Letter of Recommendation (3:1–6)
    C. The Greater Glory of New Covenant Ministry (3:7–18)
    D. The Message of Christ, the Light of the Gospel (4:1–6)
    E. The Treasure of the Gospel in Earthen Vessels (4:7–15)
    F. The Hope of Future Glory (4:16–5:10)
    G. The Ministry of Reconciliation (5:11–21)
    H. The Credentials of a Genuine Servant of God (6:1–13)
    I. An Appeal to Refuse Fellowship with Unbelievers (6:14–7:1)
    J. Final Exhortation and Rejoicing at Repentance (7:2–16)

Notes

1

2

3

4

5

6

7

Notes

8

9

10

11

12

Notes

13

14

15

16

17

18

19

Notes

20

21

22

23

24

STUDY QUESTIONS

1. Verse 3: How does Paul describe God the Father? How could knowing that help believers?

2. Verse 4: What does receiving comfort from God prepare Christians to do?

3. Verses 8–9: What did Paul experience? What was God's purpose in it?

4. Verse 12: What was Paul's confidence about his ministry?

5. Verse 14: What does Paul anticipate about the day of Christ?

6. Verses 18–20: Why is it important that preachers be men of truth and faithfulness?

7. Verse 22: What has God done for believers by the Holy Spirit (Eph. 1:13–14; 4:30)?

8. Verse 24: What should ministers be for people? What should ministers not be?

DEVOTIONAL REFLECTIONS

1. When you put your trials—past and present—next to what Paul says here, can you see any purpose, comfort, or mercy in your afflictions?

2. One result of experiencing the comfort of God is that you are able to provide comfort to others in their trials. Enduring trials and experiencing God's comfort should make you more sensitive to the afflictions of those around you. Do you know someone suffering as you once did? How can you help?

3. Paul defended his travel plans to those in Corinth. The assumptions made against Paul are shocking. Instead of thinking the best—that there would be some legitimate reason to move the apostle to change his plans—some accused him of being fickle, untrustworthy, and worldly. This should cause us to pause and evaluate how quickly we also assume the worst. Are you more prone to think the worst or the best of others?

Notes

1

2

3

4

5

6

Notes

7

8

9

10

11

12

13

14

Notes

15

16

17

STUDY QUESTIONS

1. Verses 1–2: What is one reason why Christians should not discourage each other?

2. Verse 4: What was Paul's attitude when he corrected the Corinthians in a previous letter?

3. Verses 7–8: What should the church do for a member who was put under discipline but is now repentant?

4. Verse 11: What might happen if a church fails to be merciful in its discipline?

5. Verses 14–16: What does Paul compare gospel ministry to?

6. Verse 17: What makes a true minister different from many preachers?

DEVOTIONAL REFLECTIONS

1. Discipline is necessary for the restoration of an erring brother or sister and for the purity of the church. Paul encourages Christians to use discernment and a balance between confrontation and forgiveness. He reminds us that Satan is always looking for an advantage. How do you respond to sin that you see in yourself, in others at church, and in your family members?

2. The message of the gospel is an aroma to all who hear its proclamation. To those who embrace the gospel, it is a sweet fragrance of life unto life. To those who reject it, the gospel is a stench of death unto death. Where do you stand in relation to its message?

Notes

1

2

3

4

5

6

Notes

7

8

9

10

11

12

13

Notes

14

15

16

17

18

STUDY QUESTIONS

1. Verses 1–3: What was Paul's letter of commendation? How was it written?

2. Verses 5–6: What is the sufficiency of a new covenant minister?

3. Verses 7–9: What does Paul call the old covenant ministry? Why?

4. Verse 12: What characterized Paul's preaching? What produced this?

5. Verses 13–15: What did Moses do? Why (Ex. 34:29–35)? How does Paul use this event to describe how the Jews read the Old Testament?

6. Verse 18: How do believers see the Lord's glory? How does this affect them? How have you experienced this in your own life?

DEVOTIONAL REFLECTIONS

1. Paul's attention to the superiority of the new covenant glory comes to a climax by celebrating the reality that all those who believe can behold Jesus Christ with uncovered faces. This is a remarkable and amazing benefit. Paul says that there are those even today who still read Moses with veiled hearts. One can perform religious duties and even be identified with the church, but there must be faith in order to see Christ as He is. Do you have faith to see the spiritual glory of Christ? What does it mean to experience this saving privilege?

2. The great freedom of the gospel is the access a believer has to gaze upon Christ by faith through the help of the Spirit. The result of this gaze is greater conformity to the image of Jesus Christ. People become like that which they gaze upon or see. How does this motivate you to diligently use the ordinary means of grace such as preaching? What should we pray as we prepare to worship with the church?

Notes

1

2

3

4

5

6

Notes

7

8

9

10

11

12

13

14

Notes

15

16

17

18

STUDY QUESTIONS

1. Verse 2: What must a minister of the gospel renounce? What must he aim to do?

2. Verse 4: Why are unbelievers unable to believe the gospel?

3. Verse 6: How does God save people when they hear the gospel?

4. Verses 7–10: What is often the experience of ministers? What is God's purpose in this?

5. Verses 13–15: What motivates ministers to keep preaching?

6. Verses 17–18: How does the believer's present compare to his or her future?

DEVOTIONAL REFLECTIONS

1. God is sovereign in salvation. Through the preaching of the gospel (general call) God commands the light of the glorious gospel of Christ to shine in the hearts of some hearers (effectual call). Have you experienced the gospel in your heart, or do you continue to have your eyes blinded by Satan? Experiencing the light of the gospel brings you to the knowledge of the glory of God in the face of Jesus Christ.

2. The Bible teaches about different kinds of suffering. There is suffering because of sin (David and Bathsheba). There is suffering because of someone else's sin (Achan). There is suffering for the sake of righteousness (Paul). There is suffering when the cause is not immediately discernible (Job). Paul's words here apply most directly to the latter two kinds of suffering. The only way to consider real and deep affliction as light is to see them compared to the weight of eternal glory. As you go through hardships in your life, seek God's grace to suffer well and to have an eternal perspective, focusing on those things that are not seen and are eternal.

Notes

1

2

3

4

5

6

7

8

Notes

9

10

11

12

13

14

15

Notes

16

17

18

19

20

21

1. Verse 1: To what does Paul compare our present bodies and resurrection bodies?

2. Verse 2: What is the believer's attitude toward his or her future resurrection?

3. Verses 6–8: What does Paul say about the believer on earth? About the believer after death?

4. Verses 10–11: What is one motivation for evangelism?

5. Verses 14–15: How does Christ's death change those for whom He died and rose again?

6. Verses 18–20: How does Paul describe the gospel ministry?

7. Verse 21: What great exchange did God perform in Christ to save His people?

DEVOTIONAL REFLECTIONS

1. Meditate on the future realities of the gospel. Have you learned by grace to groan to be clothed with a glorified body? Take time to consider and meditate upon all that awaits the children of God. If you have the Spirit, all this is yours in earnest already.

2. Chapter 5 closes with one of the most succinctly stated summaries of the gospel. God made Christ to be sin for His people. Sinners receive the righteousness of Christ by faith. Have you rested in the gospel? Do you know experientially what it is to be counted as righteous in God's eyes? If so, celebrate the reconciliation that is found in Christ. If you have received that reconciliation, like Paul, how can you help others to be reconciled to Him?

Notes

1

2

3

4

5

6

7

Notes

8

9

10

11

12

13

14

15

Notes

16

17

18

STUDY QUESTIONS

1. Verse 2: What does Paul mean by "now is the day of salvation"?

2. Verses 4–7: What shows that someone is a true minister of God?

3. Verses 8–10: What are some ways that the life of a minister is a paradox?

4. Verses 14–15: What duty do believers have with respect to unbelievers? Why?

5. Verses 16–18: What promises does God give? To whom are the promises given?

DEVOTIONAL REFLECTIONS

1. This chapter addresses the qualifications of a genuine ministry in contrast to a false ministry. How can the truths presented here instruct you in praying for your minister and other church officers in personal and family times of prayer?

2. Associations matter to God. Because you have received reconciliation with God it is contradictory to remain in close association with unbelievers and have your life influenced by your former way of life. In what ways should Christians give careful attention to their associations?

Notes

1

2

3

4

5

6

Notes

7

8

9

10

Notes

11

12

13

14

Notes

15

16

  1. Verse 1: How should believers respond to the promises of the last chapter?

  2. Verse 3: How does Paul express his affection for the Corinthian saints?

  3. Verse 5: What did Paul experience when he came to Macedonia?

  4. Verses 10–11: What are two kinds of sorrow over sin? What does the better one produce?

  5. Verse 15: How did the Corinthians receive Titus? Why (v. 11)?

DEVOTIONAL REFLECTIONS

1. How Christians live matters to God. In the Bible there are many motivations for pursuing holiness. Gratitude for God's grace is a chief motivation. So are the promises of God. Paul appeals to God's covenantal promise to be your God and to receive you as His sons and daughters. Being a child of God ought to affect and influence your behavior. Children often look and act like their parents. How do things stand with you?

2. When sin is confronted in your life, do you experience a sorrow for getting caught, or is there a sorrow for offending God that leads to repentance? The Christian life is one of perpetual repentance. There should be constant turning from sin unto Christ. Are you grateful that God granted you repentance to seek Him for grace to lead a life pleasing to Him? While dealing with sin is hard, a repentance that leads to salvation is never regrettable.

Notes

1

2

3

4

5

6

7

Notes

8

9

10

11

12

13

Notes

14

15

16

17

18

19

20

Notes

21

22

23

24

STUDY QUESTIONS

1. Verses 1–5: How were the Macedonian churches an example of generosity?

2. Verse 6: Why does Paul call financial giving a "grace" (see also vv. 1, 7, 19; 9:8, 14)?

3. Verse 9: How is Christ the supreme example of generosity?

4. Verse 12: What makes giving acceptable to God?

5. Verses 13–15: How should giving be directed by the principle of "equality" (or "fairness")?

6. Verse 19: What does it imply about church cooperation that this man was chosen by the churches (see also v. 23)?

7. Verses 20–21: What was Paul's concern? How did he address this concern (vv. 18–22)?

8. Verse 23: Why were these messengers of the churches "the glory of Christ"?

DEVOTIONAL REFLECTIONS

1. The truth of the gospel ought to motivate us on many levels. To think how Christ gave of Himself (v. 9) should make us ready to give of ourselves and our possessions. How should this motivate your giving?

2. Paul takes great care to remain above reproach in the matter of the collection. He knows that there might be some in Corinth suspicious of how Paul was handling the monetary funds. Instead of dismissing such suspicions as unfounded, he goes the extra mile to take precautions. How should this example direct you?

Notes

1

2

3

4

5

Notes

6

7

8

9

10

11

Notes

12

13

14

15

STUDY QUESTIONS

1. Verse 2: Why was Paul already confident of their willingness to give?

2. Verse 6: What does this saying mean with respect to financial giving?

3. Verses 7–8: What kind of giving pleases God? How does the promise about God motivate that kind of giving?

4. Verses 12–13: What is the ultimate goal of financial giving to help needy believers?

5. Verse 14: How would those who receive the gift respond?

DEVOTIONAL REFLECTIONS

1. Take time to praise God for the privilege to give. If you have children, teach them by precept and example that giving is in response to God's gifts. In times of corporate worship, be mindful that the time devoted to giving is to be an act of worship, not an intermission during worship.

2. Paul concludes his discussion on the collection with a prayer of praise to God for His indescribable gift. One of the remarkable characteristics of the apostle Paul is that he sees Christ in and behind everything. Pray to God for such a view of Christ—both His person and work—and that you never lose the wonder of God's grace in giving His only begotten Son. "Thanks be unto God for his unspeakable gift" (v. 15)!

Notes

Chapter 10

1

2

3

4

5

6

7

Notes

8

9

10

11

12

13

Notes

14

15

16

17

18

1. Verse 1: How should we be like Christ when exhorting each other?

2. Verses 4–5: What does Paul teach about the "weapons" of gospel ministry?

3. Verse 8: For what purpose does the Lord give authority to His ministers?

4. Verse 10: What criticisms of Paul did his enemies make?

5. Verse 12: Why is it foolish to compare ourselves to other people?

6. Verses 17–18: What are two good reasons not to boast about yourself?

DEVOTIONAL REFLECTIONS

1. We live in a day not much different from Paul's day in Corinth. It is easy to evaluate ministers by their charisma and appearance. Yet what matters is God's call in their life. How do you view your minister? Do you love him and pray for him, or do you compare him with leaders or preachers who are more well known?

2. Paul reminds his readers of the real battle that is waged in this life (vv. 3–5). Give attention to your life and seek after the weapons that through God's might are able to bring every thought captive to the obedience of Jesus Christ. How can you use the spiritual weapons of the Word, prayer, and the ministry of the Spirit to overthrow the imaginations and high things that are against the knowledge of God?

Notes

1

2

3

4

5

6

7

Notes

8

9

10

11

12

13

14

15

Notes

16

17

18

19

20

21

22

23

Notes

24

25

26

27

28

29

30

Notes

31

32

33

STUDY QUESTIONS

1. Verse 2: To what does Paul compare himself and the church?

2. Verses 3–4: What threatens the purity of the church's devotion to Jesus Christ?

3. Verse 6: What about Paul's ministry did his enemies seek to use against him?

4. Verses 7–9: How did Paul humbly serve the Corinthians?

5. Verses 13–15: What are Satan and his ministers capable of doing?

6. Verse 20: What kind of mistreatment do churches sometimes tolerate from leaders?

7. Verses 23–27: To what credentials did Paul point to show he was a true minister of Christ?

8. Verses 28–29: What inward trials did Paul suffer? What does this show about him?

9. Verse 31: Who does Paul invoke as his witness? Why?

10. Verses 32–33: How did Paul escape arrest in Damascus (Acts 9:23–25)?

DEVOTIONAL REFLECTIONS

1. The character and subtlety of false teachers should keep Christians watchful and discerning. The best way to identify the threats of the false teachers is to be convinced of the truthfulness of the gospel and to be single-mindedly devoted to Christ (v. 3). Failing to remain devoted to Christ can make a believer susceptible to the subtle attacks of Satan, the deceiver. How can you be vigilant and jealous to protect your exclusive devotion to Jesus Christ?

2. Paul boasted in his sufferings and in his weakness. Let Paul's boasting cause you to reflect on your own trials and afflictions. He was willing to endure hardships and even face death. It is only as you are captivated by Christ and certain of His love for you that you will have a framework by which to view your own trials properly. Reflect on what it means to be singularly devoted to Christ, even in the midst of trying circumstances.

Notes

1

2

3

4

5

6

7

Notes

8

9

10

11

12

13

Notes

14

15

16

17

18

19

20

21

STUDY QUESTIONS

1. Verses 1–4: What amazing experience did Paul report?

2. Verse 7: What did the Lord permit to happen to Paul? Why?

3. Verses 8–9: How did the Lord reply to Paul's repeated prayers? What did Paul learn from this?

4. Verse 12: What are some signs of a true apostle?

5. Verse 14: How should a minister be like a parent? What should he seek from people?

6. Verse 18: How did Titus conduct himself when visiting Corinth?

7. Verses 20–21: What did Paul fear he would find when he came to Corinth?

DEVOTIONAL REFLECTIONS

1. With one hand God gives thorns to His children, but with the other He gives sufficient grace. Whatever affliction or trial you may be enduring presently, dear believer, be sure to recognize God's sufficient supply of grace as well. Satan may intend to torment you through this thorn, but God means it for your good and His glory. What trials are you facing now? What does it mean to boast in your weaknesses so that Christ's power may be seen?

2. Paul's love to the Corinthians was simply amazing. He wrote in verse 19, "we do all things, dearly beloved, for your edifying." By the Spirit's grace, what means can you use so that you could come closer to being able to say this to your spouse, your children, your parents, and your friends?

Notes

1

2

3

4

5

6

Notes

7

8

9

10

11

Notes

12

13

14

STUDY QUESTIONS

1. Verses 1–2: What principle of the law did Paul cite (Deut. 19:15)? How did he apply it?

2. Verse 3: Who spoke through Paul? What does this imply about Paul's letters?

3. Verse 5: What must professing believers do at times? Why is this important?

4. Verse 9: How did Paul express his authentic love for the saints?

5. Verse 11: What closing exhortations does Paul give them?

6. Verse 14: How does this blessing show distinct fellowship with each person of the Trinity?

DEVOTIONAL REFLECTIONS

1. Paul closes his letter with a solemn exhortation to examine oneself. He has been scrutinized and forced into a position where he must defend his claim as an apostle of Christ. He asks his readers to scrutinize themselves. It is not enough to be associated with the church of Jesus Christ. You must examine yourself and determine whether you are in Christ or not. What are the marks of a true believer in Christ?

2. All the spiritual blessings you receive come from the love of God the Father, who planned salvation before time began. All blessings come through the grace of Jesus Christ the Mediator, who died to purchase redemption and rose again to apply it to His people. And all blessings are shared within the church by the Holy Spirit. Have you experienced the grace of Christ, the love of the Father, and the communion of the Holy Spirit? If so, then meditate upon these blessings and pray for God to increase your enjoyment of Him. If not, then turn from your sin in genuine repentance and turn to Christ in faith.